EXPANDED EDITION

Grade 2

The *Flight of the Pollinators* lesson is part of the Picture-Perfect STEM program K–2 written by the program authors and includes lessons from their award-winning series.

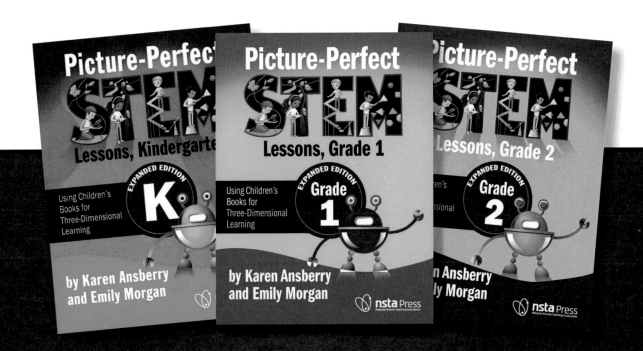

Picture-Perfect STEM Lessons, Kindergarten
Using Children's Books for Three-Dimensional Learning
EXPANDED EDITION K
by Karen Ansberry and Emily Morgan

Picture-Perfect STEM Lessons, Grade 1
Using Children's Books for Three-Dimensional Learning
EXPANDED EDITION Grade 1
by Karen Ansberry and Emily Morgan
nsta Press
National Science Teaching Association

Picture-Perfect STEM Lessons, Grade 2
...ren's ...nsional
EXPANDED EDITION Grade 2
...n Ansberry ...ly Morgan
nsta Press
National Science Teaching Association

Additional information about using the Picture Perfect Science series, including key reading strategies, NGSS connections, and the BSCS 5E instructional model can be downloaded for free at:

Flight of the Pollinators

Description

Students are introduced to the phenomenon that certain kinds of flowers are visited by certain kinds of animals. They dissect flowers to investigate what the animals are searching for inside the flowers and learn how both plants and animals benefit from the process of pollination. Finally, students develop a simple model that mimics a pollinator and use it to demonstrate plant pollination.

Alignment with the *Next Generation Science Standards*

Performance Expectations

K-2-ETS1-2: Develop a simple sketch, drawing, or physical model to illustrate how the shape of an object helps it function as needed to solve a given problem.

2-LS2-2: Develop a simple model that mimics the function of an animal in dispersing seeds or pollinating plants.

Science and Engineering Practices	Disciplinary Core Ideas	Crosscutting Concepts
Developing and Using Models Develop and/or use a model to represent amounts, relationships, relative scales (bigger, smaller), and/or patterns in the natural and designed world(s). **Obtaining, Evaluating, and Communicating Information** Read grade-appropriate texts and/or use media to obtain scientific and/or technical information to determine patterns in and/or evidence about the natural and designed world(s). Communicate information or design ideas and/or solutions with others in oral and/or written forms using models, drawings, writing, or numbers that provide details about scientific ideas, practices, and/or design solutions.	**LS2.A: Interdependent Relationships in Ecosystems** Plants depend on animals for pollination or to move their seeds around. **ETS1.B: Developing Possible Solutions** Designs can be conveyed through sketches, drawings, or physical models. These representations are useful in communicating ideas for a problem's solutions to other people.	**Structure and Function** The shape and stability of structures of natural and designed objects are related to their function(s). **Systems and System Models** Systems in the natural and designed world have parts that work together. Objects and organisms can be described in terms of their parts.

Note: The activities in this lesson will help students move toward the performance expectations listed, which is the goal after multiple activities. However, the activities will not by themselves be sufficient to reach the performance expectations.

Featured Picture Books

TITLE: **Flowers Are Calling**
AUTHOR: **Rita Gray**
ILLUSTRATOR: **Kenard Pak**
PUBLISHER: **HMH Books for Young Readers**
YEAR: **2015**
GENRE: **Narrative Information**
SUMMARY: *Beautiful artwork and poetry come together to introduce children to the wonders of pollination and the variety of pollinators.*

TITLE: **What Is Pollination?**
AUTHOR: **Bobbie Kalman**
PUBLISHER: **Crabtree Publishing**
YEAR: **2010**
GENRE: **Non-Narrative Information**
SUMMARY: *Photographs, diagrams, and straightforward text introduce a variety of pollinators and explain the importance of pollination for both the plants and the pollinators.*

Time Needed

This lesson will take several class periods. Suggested scheduling is as follows:

Session 1: Engage with *Flowers Are Calling* Read-Aloud and **Explore** with Look at a Flower—What Do You See?

Session 2: Explain with *What Is Pollination?* Read-Aloud

Session 3: Elaborate with Pollinator Model Design Challenge

Session 4: Evaluate with Pollination Presentations

Materials

For Look at a Flower—What Do You See? (per student or pair)

• Flower

  Note: Ask a local florist for flowers that are going to be discarded. Lilies, irises, daffodils, alstroemeria, tulips, or others with obvious pistils and stamens are best for this activity. Make sure that the flowers are mature so that the pistils and stamens are visible.

• Hand lens
• Cotton swab
• Piece of clear tape

For What Is Pollination? *Read-Aloud*

• Scissors
• Tape or glue

National Science Teaching Association

For Pollinator Model Design Challenge (per student)

- 5 multicolor acrylic pom-poms (0.19 in. or 5.0 mm size)
- 2 small paper cups
- 1 acrylic glove (Magic brand works well.)
- 5 Velcro dots (3/8 in. or 0.9 cm; just hooks, not loops)
- A variety of supplies to build and decorate models, such as construction paper, pipe cleaners, googly eyes, coffee filters, scissors, tape, and glue

Student Pages

- Look at a Flower—What Do You See?
- What Is Pollination?
- Pollinator Model Design Challenge
- 4-3-2-1 Pollination Presentation Rubric
- STEM Everywhere

Background for Teachers

The Natural Resources Conservation Service estimates that 75% of the world's plants and about 35% of the world's crops depend on animals for *pollination* (NRCS 2016). Some scientists estimate that animal *pollinators* are responsible for one in every three bites of food we eat! Pollination is critical to the sexual reproduction of flowering plants. Most flowers have male and female parts. The *stamen* (male part) makes a powder called *pollen*. The *pistil* (female part) must receive pollen to make seeds. The pistil has three parts: the *stigma*, *style*, and *ovary*. When pollen from a stamen reaches a stigma, the flower has been *pollinated*. The pollen travels down the style to the ovary. Inside the ovary are *ovules*. After pollination, the flower's petals fall off, the ovaries become fruit, and the ovules become seeds.

There are different ways flowering plants are pollinated. Some flowers can *self-pollinate*, which means pollen from the stamen moves to the pistil of the same flower. Flowers that self-pollinate have male and female parts close together. Sunflowers are an example of a flower that can self-pollinate. *Wind pollination* occurs when the wind carries pollen from one flower to another. Flowers that are pollinated by wind produce large amounts of tiny pollen grains, and much of the pollen does not make it to another flower. Wind-pollinated flowers are usually not fragrant and do not produce nectar because they do not need to attract pollinators. Many trees and grasses are pollinated by wind. *Cross-pollination* occurs when an animal moves pollen from one flower to another flower of the same species. Animals that move the pollen, such as insects, birds, and

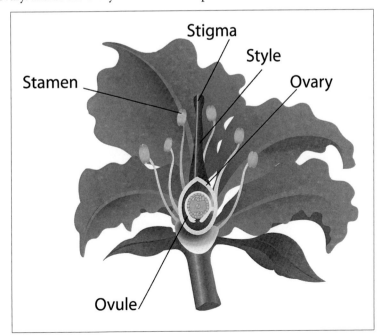

FLOWER DIAGRAM

bats, are called pollinators. Pollinators visit flowers to find food. Many of them eat the nectar produced by flowers. Some pollinators, such as bees, even eat the pollen itself. In their quest for nectar, these animals get pollen stuck on their bodies. When the animals visit other flowers of the same species, some of the pollen falls off their bodies onto the flowers. Thus, the animals unknowingly become pollinators.

Scientists have discovered that many pollinators are in danger. Strong evidence shows a decline in both the number and the diversity of some pollinators, including bees, butterflies, bats, and hummingbirds. Pesticides, disease, habitat loss, invasive plants, and climate change are thought to be the primary reasons these vital organisms are disappearing. One of the most important pollinators, the honeybee, is experiencing colony collapse disorder (CCD). CCD is a syndrome characterized by a nearly abandoned colony that includes dead bee bodies and lacks adult worker bees but still has a live queen and, usually, immature bees and honey. No cause for CCD has been scientifically proven, but some evidence points to a combination of factors, including parasitic mites and the overuse of a certain type of pesticide.

In this lesson, students are engaged in the crosscutting concept (CCC) of structure and function as they model the parts of plants and animals that make pollination possible. They also engage in the CCC of systems and system models as they learn that pollination is a system composed of parts that work together, benefitting both the animals and plants involved. They use the science and engineering practice (SEP) of developing and using models as they create a model that demonstrates this relationship. The SEP of obtaining, evaluating, and communicating information appears throughout the lesson as they read about pollination and then use what they have learned to explain how their model demonstrates the process.

Pollination is a key concept in understanding the interdependent relationships in ecosystems. The *Framework* suggests that students in grades K–2 learn that plants depend on animals for pollination. This understanding is crucial to comprehending the impact of pollinators on our ecosystems. The factors that make up a healthy ecosystem are addressed in more depth in grades 3–5.

Learning Progressions

Below are the disciplinary core idea (DCI) grade band endpoints for grades K–2 and 3–5. These are provided to show how student understanding of the DCIs in this lesson will progress in future grade levels.

DCIs	Grades K–2	Grades 3–5
LS2.A: Interdependent Relationships in Ecosystems	• Plants depend on animals for pollination or to move their seeds around.	• A healthy ecosystem is one in which multiple species of different types are each able to meet their needs in a relatively stable web of life.
ETS1.B: Developing Possible Solutions	• Designs can be conveyed through sketches, drawings, or physical models. These representations are useful in communicating ideas for a problem's solutions to other people.	• At whatever stage, communicating with peers about proposed solutions is an important part of the design process, and shared ideas can lead to improved designs.

Source: Willard, T., ed. 2015. *The NSTA quick-reference guide to the* NGSS: *Elementary school.* Arlington, VA: NSTA Press.

National Science Teaching Association

engage

Flowers Are Calling Read-Aloud

Connecting to the Common Core
Reading: Informational Text
CRAFT AND STRUCTURE: 2.5

**Inferring**

Show students the cover of *Flowers Are Calling* and introduce the author, Rita Gray, and the illustrator, Kenard Pak. *Ask*

? What do you think the title *Flowers Are Calling* means? Whom or what do you think the flowers are calling? (Answers will vary.)

? Do you notice any animals on the cover? (Students will likely notice the bee, butterfly, and hummingbird on the cover.)

? What do you notice about the colors and shapes of the flowers on the cover? (The flowers are different colors and shapes.)

? Why do you think flowers are different colors and shapes? (Answers will vary.)

Synthesizing

Tell students that, as you read, you would like them think about what the title *Flowers Are Calling* means. Read the book aloud, stopping after the page that says, "They're calling some children to look again." Then *ask*

? Have your ideas changed about what the title *Flowers Are Calling* means? (Students should realize that the flowers are attracting different animals in different ways.)

? What animals were the flowers "calling" in the book? (butterfly, bumblebee, hummingbird, honeybee, beetle, bee fly, pollen wasp, moth, and bat)

? What do all of these animals have in common? (They all fly, they are attracted to flowers, they eat nectar, etc.)

? Have you ever seen any of the animals in the book in the wild? (Answers will vary.)

? Why do animals visit flowers? (Animals eat the flowers' nectar.)

? Why would flowers need to attract animals? (Answers will vary.)

OBSERVING FLOWER STRUCTURES IN THE CLASSROOM

explore

Look at a Flower—What Do You See?

Connecting to the Common Core
Reading: Informational Text
INTEGRATION OF KNOWLEDGE AND IDEAS: K.7, 1.7, 2.7

Give each student or pair of students a flower, a hand lens, a cotton swab, and the Look at a Flower—What Do You See? student page. Have students draw a detailed sketch of the flower. (Students do not necessarily need to know the vocabulary associated with the different flower parts at this time.) Turn to pages 28–30 in *Flowers Are Calling*, which are titled "Look at a Flower—What Do You See?" As you read the sections aloud, have students listen for what each characteristic has to do with "calling" animals to visit the flower. Point out the illustrations that accompany each section, and explain that the illustrator provided this art to help the reader better understand each characteristic. After reading each section, have students observe the colors, patterns, shape, and smell of their own flowers and fill in their observations in the table. (*Note*: Time of opening is not on the student page because that characteristic cannot be observed during class time. However, read the paragraph and discuss so students know that time of opening is also an important factor in attracting certain animals.) Later, you may want to take students outside to observe flower structures on flowering plants found in your schoolyard. In this way, students can compare how the same flower structures may look different on different plants.

> **SEP: Obtaining, Evaluating, and Communicating Information**
> Read grade-appropriate text to obtain scientific information and determine patterns about the natural world.

OBSERVING FLOWER STRUCTURES IN THE SCHOOLYARD

COLLECTING POLLEN

National Science Teaching Association

Tell students that the reason the flowers were "calling" to the animals has to do with a special powdery substance inside the flower. Encourage them to look carefully to find the powder. When they find it, they should rub some off with a cotton swab and smear it in the corresponding box on the paper. Then have students place a piece of clear tape over the powder to hold it in place. Tell students that, in the next part of the lesson, they will find out what this mysterious powder is and why it is so important. (Some students may know that the powder is called *pollen*, but assure them that there is much to learn about why it is there and what it does.)

> **CCC: Systems and System Models**
> Organisms can be described in terms of their parts

 explain

What Is Pollination? Read-Aloud

Connecting to the Common Core
Language
VOCABULARY ACQUISITION AND USE: 2.6

Cloze

Show students the cover of *What Is Pollination?* by Bobbie Kalman. Tell them this book can help them discover what that mysterious powder is and what it has to do with the flowers and the animals in *Flowers Are Calling*. Give students the *What Is Pollination?* student page. Directions for students are as follows:

1. Cut out the cards in the boxes.
2. Read the paragraph, and fill in each blank with the card you think belongs there.

3. Listen carefully while your teacher reads the book *What Is Pollination?*
4. After reviewing the paragraph as a class, move the cards if necessary. Then glue or tape them on the page.
5. On the back, draw a picture of what *pollination* means.

> **SEP: Obtaining, Evaluating, and Communicating Information**
> Read grade-appropriate text to obtain scientific information and determine patterns about the natural world.

The paragraph should read as follows:

Pollen is the fine powder at the center of most flowers. When it moves from one flower to another flower of the same kind, **pollination** takes place. Flowers must be pollinated to make **fruits** and **seeds**. Animals that carry pollen from one flower to another are called **pollinators**. They are not pollinating flowers on purpose. Most animals visit flowers because they are looking for **nectar**!

Connecting to the Common Core
Reading: Informational Text
CRAFT AND STRUCTURE: 2.5

Questioning

Ask

? Do pollinators know that they are helping the plants? (no)

? Why do pollinators visit flowers? (to get nectar or food for themselves)

? How do both the plants and pollinators benefit from pollination? (The plants get their pollen moved to other flowers, which allows them to make new plants, and the pollinators get food.)

CCC: Systems and System Models
Systems in the natural world have parts that work together.

Explain that pollinators and plants work together as a system. Systems in the natural world have parts that work together. For example, on page 11 of *What Is Pollination?*, students can see how the shape of a hummingbird's beak works with the shape of tubular flowers. On page 17, they can see how the furry body of a bumblebee works to carry sticky pollen produced by the plant.

On page 31, the author writes, "Each time you bite into an apple, pear, or vegetable, say a silent 'Thank you' to the pollinators that made it possible." *Ask*

? Why should we thank pollinators? (If plants were not pollinated, fruits and vegetables would not grow.)

? Why are pollinators in danger? (People are building in wilderness areas, which causes animals, including pollinators, to lose their homes and food. Pesticides and diseases are killing many pollinating insects.)

? What can we do to help pollinators? (Tell people why pollinators are important. Grow native flowers at home or school. Plant a vegetable or other garden.)

elaborate

Pollinator Model Design Challenge

Tell students that you have a challenge for each of them—to design and build a model that helps demonstrate how pollinators move pollen from one place to another. They will be using the following materials to build their models:

- 5 small pom-poms to represent pollen
- 2 small paper cups to represent two of the same type of flower

MODEL OF A POLLINATOR

- 1 acrylic glove on which they can tape or glue the following materials to make their models (see photo):
  - 5 small Velcro dots to represent the structures on the pollinator that pollen sticks to
  - Other materials to add more structures and details to their model: construction paper, pipe cleaners, googly eyes, coffee filters, tape, and glue

Their models will need to transfer pom-poms (pollen) from one cup (flower) to the other cup (flower). They may decorate the cups (e.g., add petals) if they would like to make them look more like flowers.

Tell students that before they begin, you want to give them the opportunity to see some pollinators in action. Explain that you have a clip from a movie called *Wings of Life* (see "Websites") that a filmmaker named Louis Schwartzberg made to teach people about pollination. Tell them that as they watch, you would like them to look for different types of pollinators, observe their different body parts, and watch how the pollinators interact with flowers.

Questioning

After watching the video, *ask*

? What pollinators were featured in the video? (hummingbirds, bees, butterflies, and bats)

? How did they get from flower to flower? (by flying)

? Why were these animals visiting the flowers? (to get nectar)

? What body parts help them get to the nectar (Wings help them fly to the flowers, hummingbirds' long beaks can go deep inside flowers, bats and butterflies have long tongues to slurp nectar, bees' bodies are small enough to go inside many flowers, etc.)

> **SEP: Developing and Using Models**
> Develop and use a model to demonstrate relationships in the natural world.
>
> **CCC: Structure and Function**
> The shape of structures of natural objects are related to their functions.

Then give each student the Pollinator Model Design Challenge student page. Some suggestions for pollinators to model are bees, wasps, butterflies, moths, flies, beetles, hummingbirds, and bats. Have each student look through an online photo gallery (see "Websites") to choose a pollinator to model, record it online, print out a photo, and attach it to the student page. The photos will be used for reference as students make their models.

Next, they will describe how the real pollinator gets food from the flower and how the model pol-

linator will show this. They will also describe the parts of the real pollinator's body that the pollen sticks to and how the model pollinator will show this. Finally, they will explain how both plants and pollinators benefit from their interaction and how humans benefit from pollination. Students will use the photo and this information to help them design and build their models.

evaluate

Pollination Presentations

Synthesizing

After students have completed their models, pass out the 4-3-2-1 Pollination Presentation Rubric student page. Students should use the information from the Pollinator Model Design Challenge student page to help them with their presentations. You may consider having students present their models to an outside audience such as a local park official or nature expert.

Give students time to practice, then have them either give their presentations live or record them to be shown later. They must include the following information:

- A demonstration of how the pollinator moves pollen from one flower to another
- A description of the body parts that the pollinator uses to get food from the flower and the body parts that the pollen sticks to
- An explanation of how both plants and pollinators benefit from pollination
- An explanation of how humans benefit from pollination

Students can also share what they might do to improve their models. Use the rubric to evaluate their presentations.

STEM Everywhere

Give students the STEM Everywhere student page as a way to involve their families and extend their learning. They can do the activity with an adult helper and share their results with the class. If students do not have access to the internet at home, you may choose to have them complete this activity at school.

Opportunities for Differentiated Instruction

This box lists questions and challenges related to the lesson that students may select to research, investigate, or innovate. Students may also use the questions as examples to help them generate their own questions. These questions can help you move your students from the teacher-directed investigation to engaging in the science and engineering practices in a more student-directed format.

Extra Support

For students who are struggling to meet the lesson objectives, provide a question and guide them in the process of collecting research or help them design procedures or solutions.

Extensions

For students with high interest or who have already met the lesson objectives, have them choose a question (or pose their own question), conduct their own research, and design their own procedures or solutions.

After selecting one of the questions in the box or formulating their own question, students can individually or collaboratively make predictions, design investigations or surveys to test their predictions, collect evidence, devise explanations, design solutions, or examine related resources. They can communicate their findings through a science notebook, at a poster session or gallery walk, or by producing a media project.

Research

Have students brainstorm researchable questions:

? What kinds of plants would attract pollinators to your yard or schoolyard?

? Which crops in our area depend on pollinators?

? Which pollinators are in danger, and what can we do to help?

Continued

Opportunities for Differentiated Instruction (continued)

Investigate

Have students brainstorm testable questions to be solved through science or math:

? What are some common pollinators that visit our schoolyard?

? How many of the foods that I eat in a day require animal pollinators? (Keep a tally of how many times you eat vegetables, fruits, or nuts—or foods made using those products—in a day.)

? Which plants seem to attract the most pollinators in our schoolyard?

Innovate

Have students brainstorm problems to be solved through engineering:

? Can we build a feeder to attract hummingbirds to our schoolyard?

? Can we design a flower garden (either on a plot of land or in pots) to attract butterflies?

? Can we design a vegetable garden (either on a plot of land or in pots) to help pollinators?

Reference

 NRCS (Natural Resources Conservation Service). 2016. Insects and pollinators. U.S. Department of Agriculture. *www.nrcs.usda.gov/wps/portal/nrcs/main/national/plantsanimals/pollinate*

Websites

 National Geographic "Gold Dusters" Pollinator Photo Gallery *www.nationalgeographic.com/magazine/article/pollinators*

 Penn State University Department of Entomology: Pollinator Image Gallery *https://ento.psu.edu/research/centers/pollinators/resources-and-outreach/pollinator-media*

 U.S. Department of Agriculture: "Bee a Friend to Pollinators" (brochure) *https://nrcspad.sc.egov.usda.gov/distributioncenter/product.aspx?ProductID=849*

 "The Beauty of Pollination: Wings of Life" (video) *https://video.disney.com/watch/the-beauty-of-pollination-wings-of-life-4da84833e06fd54fff590f49*

More Books to Read

Bersani, S. 2015. *Achoo! Why pollen counts.* Mount Pleasant, SC: Arbordale Publishing.
Summary: A cute storyline about a baby black bear that is allergic to pollen not only teaches readers about pollen allergies but also explains how vital this fine powder is to the animals and plants in the forest.

Fleming, C. 2020. *Honeybee: The busy life of apis mellifera.* New York: Neal Porter Books.
Summary: This detailed introduction to the life of a honeybee is full of intriguing facts about one of our most important pollinators.

Konicek-Moran, R. 2016. *From flower to fruit.* Arlington, VA: NSTA Kids.
Summary: Rich illustrations and an engaging narrative draw the reader into the world of botany. The book introduces the parts of a flower, the process of pollination, and the production of fruit. It includes activities and background information for parents and teachers.

Marsh, L. 2016. *National Geographic Readers: Bees*. Washington, DC: National Geographic Kids.
Summary: A straightforward nonfiction book about bees, illustrated with stunning National Geographic photos.

Morgan, E. 2019. *Next time you see a bee*. Arlington, VA: NSTA Press.
Summary: Simple text and gorgeous photographs reveal the physical features that allow bees to collect and spread pollen. In addition to honeybees, this book describes many North American native bees and discusses why they are threatened (and how readers can help).

Pattison, D. 2019. *Pollen: Darwin's 130-year prediction*. Little Rock, AR: Mims House.
Summary: This fascinating true story reveals how Charles Darwin's prediction that a certain species of orchid on Madagascar was pollinated by giant moths would not be tested until a century later.

Pryor, K. 2019. *Bea's bees*. Chesapeake Bay, MD: Schiffer Kids.
Summary: Beatrix discovers a wild bee nest on her walk home from school. When the nest goes silent, Bea is determined to find out how she can help. End matter includes information on conserving bees.

Rich, S. 2014. *Mrs. Carter's butterfly garden*. Arlington, VA: NSTA Press.
Summary: In this story of how former First Lady Rosalynn Carter started a front-yard project that grew into a butterfly-friendly trail through her hometown of Plains, Georgia, students will learn why having welcoming spaces for butterflies is good for people and how to create their own butterfly gardens at home or school.

Slade, S. 2010. *What if there were no bees?: A book about the grassland ecosystem*. North Mankato, MN: Picture Window Books.
Summary: Part of the Food Chain Reactions series, this book highlights the importance of bees to the ecosystem. By addressing the question "What if there were no bees?," the reader learns these insects are a keystone species because many other species would likely become extinct without them.

Name: _____

Look at a Flower— What Do You See?

1. Observe the flower carefully. Draw a picture that shows its shape, colors, patterns, and parts.

[ ]

2. Listen as your teacher reads about each characteristic of a flower, then record the observations for your flower.

Characteristic	Observation
Color	
Pattern	
Shape	
Smell	

3. Look for the powdery substance in the center of your flower. Use a cotton swab to smear some in the box below and tape it in place.

What Is Pollination?

_____ is the fine powder at the center of most flowers. When it moves from one flower to another flower of the same kind, _____ takes place. Flowers must be pollinated to make _____ and _____. Animals that carry pollen from one flower to another are called _____. They are not pollinating flowers on purpose. Most animals visit flowers because they are looking for _____!

Directions: Cut out the cards below and place them in the paragraph above. Then listen as your teacher reads the book *What Is Pollination?*

fruits	**pollen**	**nectar**
pollination	**seeds**	**pollinators**

Name: _____

Pollinator Model Design Challenge

Challenge: Design a model of a pollinator that can be used to demonstrate how it moves pollen from one flower to another while getting food.

Directions: Choose a real pollinator as an inspiration for your model. Then design your model using the materials provided.

Real Pollinator	Model Pollinator
Name and photo	Labeled sketch
How does the pollinator get food from the flower?	How will your model show this?
What parts of the pollinator's body does the pollen stick to?	How will your model show this?

1. How do both plants and pollinators benefit from pollination?

   Plants get _____

   Pollinators get _____

2. How do humans benefit from pollination?

_____

Name: _____

4~3~2~1
Pollination Presentation Rubric

Demonstrate the model of a pollinator that you designed. Your presentation should include the following:

4 Points: A demonstration of how your model pollinator moves pollen from one flower to another

4 3 2 1 0

3 Points: A description of the body parts that your model pollinator uses to get food from the flower and the body parts that the pollen sticks to

3 2 1 0

2 Points: An explanation of how both plants and pollinators benefit from pollination

2 1 0

1 Point: An explanation of how humans benefit from pollination

1 0

Score: _____/10

National Science Teaching Association

Name: _____

STEM Everywhere

At school, we have been learning about **pollination**. We learned that plants depend on animals to move their pollen. These animals are called **pollinators**. Both plants and pollinators benefit from this relationship. To find out more, ask your learner questions such as:

- What did you learn?
- What was your favorite part of the lesson?
- What are you still wondering?

At home, you can watch a video together called "RoboBees to the Rescue" about how **roboticists,** or engineers who design robots, at Harvard University are designing a robotic bee to pollinate plants.

 Search "RoboBees to the Rescue" on *www.pbslearningmedia.org* to find the video at *www.pbslearningmedia.org/resource/arct14.sci. nvrobobee/robobees-to-the-rescue.*

After you watch the video, you can design your own robot that is based on a different pollinator, such as a butterfly, hummingbird, beetle, moth, or bat.

Sketch of Real Pollinator	Sketch of Robot Pollinator